HUMAN RIGHTS
FOR ALL

By Jilly Hunt

ADLINES BEYOND THE HEADLINES BEYOND THE HEAD

capstone

To contact Capstone Global Library, please call 800-747-4992, or visit our web site www.mycapstone.com

Edited by Adrian Vigliano
Designed by Philippa Jenkins
Original illustrations © Capstone Global Library Limited 2018
Illustrated by Oxford Designers and Illustrators
Picture research by Morgan Walters
Production by Tori Abraham
Originated by Capstone Global Library Ltd

21 20 19 18 17
10 9 8 7 6 5 4 3 2 1

Library of Congress Cataloging-in-Publication Data
Library of Congress Cataloging-in-Publication Data is available on the Library of Congress website.

ISBN: 978-1-4846-4141-5 (library hardcover)
ISBN: 978-1-4846-4145-3 (paperback)
ISBN: 978-1-4846-4149-1 (eBook PDF)

This book has been officially leveled using the F&P Text Level Gradient™ Levelling System.

Acknowledgments
We would like to thank the following for permission to reproduce photographs: Alamy: Ashley Cooper, 26, 27, Black Star, 30, Friedrich Stark, 22, Matthew Chattle, 32, Vickie Flores, 29; Capstone Press: Philippa Jenkins, map 1, 14, 36, ipad 5, 7, 15, 17, 18, 20, 28, 33, 36, 39; Getty Images: Allison Joyce, 23, Arne Hodalic, 15, The White House / Handout, 19, Yawar Nazir, 34; iStockphoto: Dangubic, 21; Newscom: ANTONIO COTRIM/EPA, 31, Antonio Masiello/ NurPhoto/Sipa U, 41, KIM HONG-JI/REUTERS, 43, LUC GNAGO/REUTERS/, 38, MICHAEL KOOREN / POOL/EPA, 7, Zakir Hossain Chowdhury/NurPhoto, 25; Shutterstock: 1000 Words, design element throughout, Cover, Aleksandr Lutcenko, 39, carballo, 40, Dietmar Temps, top 5, 6, ESB Professional, (classroom) Cover, Everett Historical, bottom 5, 11, 20, Featureflash Photo Agency, 33, franco lucato, 17, John Gomez, 9, journeykei, 4, JStone, 18, kafeinkolik, 37, Lesterman, 12, Mangostar, 1, Mila Supinskaya Glashchenko, 28, Morphart Creation, 10, StanislavBeloglazov, 8, Steffen Foerster, 13, Sura Nualpradid, 16

We would like to thank Michelle Fournier, Interpretive Naturalist, Chippewa Nature Center, Midland, MI, USA, for her invaluable help in the preparation of this book.

Every effort has been made to contact copyright holders of material reproduced in this book. Any omissions will be rectified in subsequent printings if notice is given to the publisher.

All the Internet addresses (URLs) given in this book were valid at the time of going to press. However, due to the dynamic nature of the Internet, some addresses may have changed, or sites may have changed or ceased to exist since publication. While the author and publisher regret any inconvenience this may cause readers, no responsibility for any such changes can be accepted by either the author or the publisher.

CONTENTS

Some words are shown in bold, **like this**. You can
find out what they mean by looking in the glossary.

Chapter 1

WHAT'S BEYOND THE HEADLINES ABOUT HUMAN RIGHTS?

"CHILD SLAVERY SPARKS OUTRAGE"

"PRESIDENT QUESTIONED ON HUMAN RIGHTS"

"CONCERN FOR HUMAN RIGHTS"

We've all seen headlines like this about human rights. But how much do we really know about this issue?

Human rights start with accepting that every person deserves to be treated equally. It means that people should not be treated differently because of the color of their skin, or their gender, religion, or language. Human rights means that everybody is born free and not into slavery.

For centuries people have argued in favor of human rights. The ancient Greek **philosopher** Socrates (470/469–399 BC) wrote that human rights were part of natural justice or natural law. People argued against human rights abuses, such as the Transatlantic Slave Trade. People continue to argue against human rights abuses that are happening in the world today.

Around 6 million Jews were killed in Nazi **concentration camps** during WWII. The Nazis attempted to completely wipe out the Jewish people. An attempt such as this is now known as genocide. This photo shows a pile of Holocaust victims' shoes.

International Agreement

After **World War II**, world leaders wanted to unite to try to stop any more wars from happening. In 1945, 50 countries joined together to form the **United Nations (UN)**. These nations also wanted to protect people's human rights. The horrific human rights abuses committed by the Nazis against Jews in WWII had not been forgotten. In 1948, countries of the United Nations agreed a statement of the rights that every human deserved. This statement is called the Universal Declaration of Human Rights or UDHR.

Prisoners at a Nazi concentration camp during WWII ▽

Human rights includes the right for all children to get an education.

The Universal Declaration of Human Rights declares that:

"all human beings are born free and equal in dignity and rights and are entitled to the rights and freedoms set out in the Declaration without discrimination on the grounds of race, color, sex, language, political opinion, or religion."

South Africa used to have a segregation policy that discriminated against people because of their race. This was a violation of human rights. ▼

Free Will

An important part of human rights is the idea of free will. A person shouldn't be forced into doing something against his or her free will. Human rights abuses often involve someone trying to control another person. For example, practices such as slavery or forcing a person to work against his or her will are human rights abuses.

DID YOU KNOW?

South Africa has increased the number of human rights in its laws including the right to use the language of an individual's choice. This means a person is not forced into speaking an "official" language.

GOOD NEWS

In 2016, the ICC convicted Jean-Pierre Bemba Gombo, the former Vice President of the Democratic Republic of the Congo, for war crimes. The ICC relied on help from member states. The Belgian government arrested him, and the Portuguese authorities monitored his bank accounts to discover when and where money was withdrawn.

Progress with Human Rights

The protection of human rights has moved on since the introduction of the UDHR. The UN has set up a Commission on Human Rights which investigates large-scale human rights issues. The International Criminal Court (ICC) aims to try cases related to war crimes, **genocide**, and crimes against humanity. The court can accuse even current leaders with a crime but they don't have the power to actually arrest the person. The ICC, therefore, relies upon other heads of states and governments to arrest and hand over wanted people. This hasn't always happened. For example, Sudan's President, Omar Hassan al-Bashir, is wanted by the ICC. He is thought to have committed crimes during the conflict in the Darfur region of Sudan. However, other countries have ignored the arrest warrant.

THINK ABOUT IT

Should we all have the same rights? In prison, prisoners lose some of their rights, mainly their right to freedom but also their right to vote. Do you think criminals should have the same rights as everyone else?

Chapter 2

WHAT'S BEYOND THE HEADLINES ABOUT THE RIGHT TO FREEDOM?

The right to freedom and to free will are key elements of human rights. Slavery is when a person's freedom and right to free will are taken away. Slavery takes different forms. When one person "owns" another person, as though they were a piece of property, it is called chattel slavery.

DID YOU KNOW?

It is estimated that 5.7 million children are victims of child slavery.

Sometimes children find themselves trapped in bonded labor because of their family's poverty.

People are trying to stop modern-day slavery by protesting to their governments.

Bonded, forced, or debt labor is when a person's labor is promised for a debt. Very often, this debt can never be repaid. For example, migrant workers smuggled into a new country might have promised their labor to repay their transportation costs. However, they may find it impossible to ever repay their debt. They are deliberately given a very low wage, from which the cost of their food and lodgings are deducted. They are trapped. Others find themselves stuck in forced labor because their employer has confiscated their passport. Women may find themselves, in effect, sold into slavery through a forced marriage.

GOOD NEWS

The photographer and blogger Brandon Stanton has raised over two million dollars to help fight bonded labor in Pakistan. He was shocked at stories about people who had no choice but to borrow from dishonest people. One man borrowed 5,000 rupees from the owners of a brick kiln. He planned to pay back the loan by working at their kiln for 15 to 20 days. When his time was up, the owners told him that he owed 11,000 rupees in food and lodging costs. He had no choice but to go back to work to pay off the new amount. But the longer he stayed and worked, the more he owed.

Is Slavery Legal?

Slavery is illegal in every country in the world. But it still happens in secret, even in developed countries such as the United Kingdom. It is thought that there are still about 21 million people who are victims of forced labor. This is more slaves than ever before.

History of Slavery

Looking back over thousands of years, the Ancient Greeks and Romans had slaves. Their slaves were often people who had been defeated by the Greeks or Romans. Some of these slaves were well-educated people, so they were made to work in trade or banking. They wouldn't have any political rights and could be bought, sold, and beaten by their master.

The Transatlantic Slave Trade

The Transatlantic Slave Trade is perhaps the most well known. This form of slavery started around 1500. People were treated as property, as though they were not even human.

This 1865 engraving shows a Persian man who has been enslaved.

Some African leaders captured people to be slaves. Captured people were taken to holding pens on the coast until they could be sold to European ship captains. Once sold, enslaved people were chained up inside ships for weeks or months as they made the journey across the Atlantic. The average space for each slave was 6 feet (183 centimeters) long, 16 inches (41 cm) wide and about 3 feet (91 cm) high. People were unable to stand up or turn over and often died in this position. Slaves were at risk of diseases, abuse by their captors, and attack by pirates. About 10 to 20 percent of these captive people died on the journey.

Once at their destination, perhaps in the U.S., Brazil, or the Caribbean, the slaves were sold. European countries such as Britain, Spain, and Portugal ran **plantations** growing crops such as cotton, tobacco, or sugar. Lots of slaves were wanted to do the hard manual work cheaply.

Many enslaved people were forced to work in the cotton industry.

Chapter 3

WHAT'S BEYOND THE HEADLINES ABOUT THE RIGHTS OF A CHILD?

Human rights apply to everyone and there are special ones for children. The rights of a child apply to everyone under 18 years old. Children's rights try to ensure that children are kept safe to live a happy life with their family. For example, children have the right to be protected from being hurt and mistreated in body or mind. No one is allowed to punish children in a cruel or harmful way.

DID YOU KNOW?

The UN has a division that specifically focuses on children, called UNICEF. It was set up in 1946 after World War II.

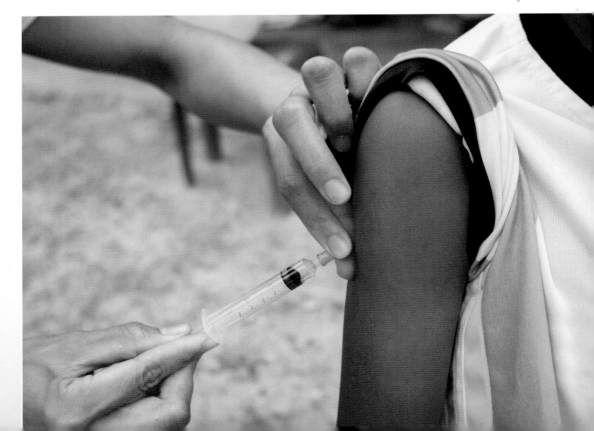

Children have the right to the best health care possible. This child is being given a vaccination. ▼

Child Labor

Children have the right to play and rest. If they do work, they have the right to be protected from work that harms them and is bad for their health or education. They have the right to be safe at work and to be paid fairly. This is what is supposed to happen. But in many parts of the world, such as in Africa or Central Asia, children are forced to work. There are numerous examples of children put to work in dangerous environments. Some children are made to work in mines where crawling in small spaces leads to spinal injuries. Others work long hours, perhaps sewing footballs or clothes, in a workplace that is unclean and poorly lit. Their health is likely to be affected and they are more likely to become ill.

Children around the world do different types of tasks to help their families. But all children have the right to be protected from harmful labor. ▼

GOOD NEWS

In Sept 2016, the United Nations' Committee on the Rights of the Child met with governments, experts, and non-governmental organizations. They wanted to discuss ways to protect children from environmental harm such as air pollution.

DID YOU KNOW?

There are over 218 million child laborers. An estimated 126 million of these children do hazardous work.

Children and War

Children have the right to protection and freedom from war. Children under 15 years old cannot be forced to join an army or take part in war. Yet, in some parts of the world, they are. For example, in the Democratic Republic of the Congo in Africa, children as young as four years old are forced to fight. Many are abducted by armed groups and are abused. Others join thinking that they will earn money, which they need to pay for school uniform and books.

Countries Where Children Are Affected by Armed Conflict

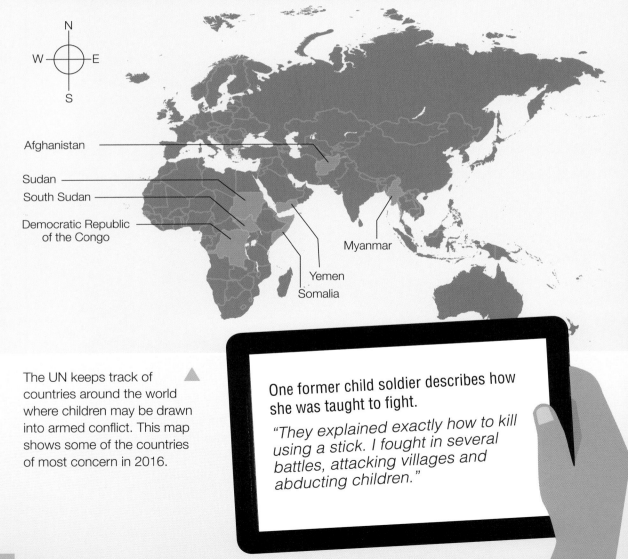

The UN keeps track of countries around the world where children may be drawn into armed conflict. This map shows some of the countries of most concern in 2016.

One former child soldier describes how she was taught to fight.

"They explained exactly how to kill using a stick. I fought in several battles, attacking villages and abducting children."

Why Are Children Made to Be Soldiers?

In times of conflict, government armies or armed groups need as many fighters as they can get to try to win their battles. Children can be easier to persuade to join than adults and are easier to abduct and force into fighting. Sometimes children get separated from their families in the chaos that comes with conflict. These children are very vulnerable and have no adults to protect them.

Where Are Child Soldiers Fighting?

The UN are concerned by seven countries found to be using children in their armed forces. These are Afghanistan, Democratic Republic of the Congo, Myanmar, Somalia, South Sudan, Sudan, and Yemen. All these countries have now signed agreements to put an end to the use of children in conflict. However, these agreements only involve the official armies, not all the armed groups they are fighting.

Children may be forced into fighting or they might feel they have no other options.

THINK ABOUT IT

Most government forces around the world don't recruit people under 18 years old, but some still do including the UK, Myanmar, and Afghanistan. What do you think about this? In other countries, including the U.S., those under 18 years old are not allowed to join the forces. However, in recent years, children have been recruited to take part in programs such as the U.S. Army's "Future Soldier Program." Is that right?

Right to an Education

The right of children to receive a good quality education is seen as a very important right. Education can help children to escape poverty. In 2016, the UN's education branch, UNESCO, reported that 263 million children and adolescents were not attending school. That is roughly the same as a quarter of the population of Europe. There are a variety of reasons why a child might not attend school. For example, 61.9 million children do not go to school because they live in conflict areas. Other children don't go because of religious or cultural beliefs. Sometimes poverty forces children into working to help support their families.

Girls are more likely than boys not to go to school because they are needed to help at home. Nine million girls in sub-Saharan Africa will never attend school. ▼

Working for Change

The UN is working to try to improve the situation. In 2015, they announced their global education goals. These goals include ensuring that all girls and boys complete free, quality primary and secondary education by 2030. Another goal is for girls and boys to get equal access to education.

GOOD NEWS

This graph shows that the global number of out-of-school children and youths has decreased between 2000 and 2014.

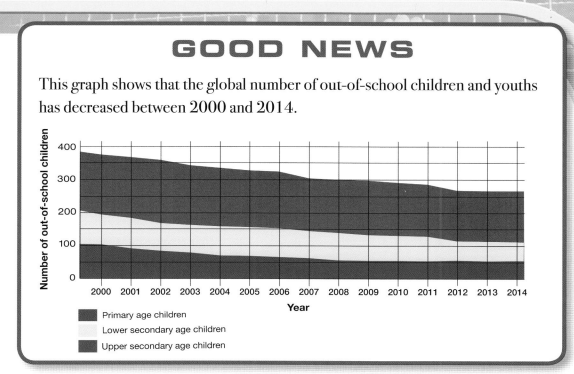

Many children are not able to receive upper secondary education. Instead they must go to work. ▼

Viewpoint:

Emmanuel Amon lives in Malawi, Africa. His parents couldn't afford to let him go to school and he started work when he was 5 years old. He woke at 4:00 a.m. every day to start a long day's work on a tobacco farm. He was sick all the time because of the thick dust and the chemicals used.

THINK ABOUT IT

Why do people think it is important for all children to have the right to an education?

CASE STUDY:

Malala Yousafzai

At just 17 years old, Malala Yousafzai is the youngest person ever to receive the Nobel Prize for Peace. She won the prize for her "struggle against the suppression of children and young people and for the right of all children to education." She was born in 1997 in northwestern Pakistan. She came to the world's attention in 2009 when she began blogging about her life under the Taliban. The Taliban are an **extremist** Muslim group that believe in very strict laws and use violence to enforce them. In 2009, the Taliban banned girls from receiving an education. Malala wrote about her feelings and said she was afraid to go to school.

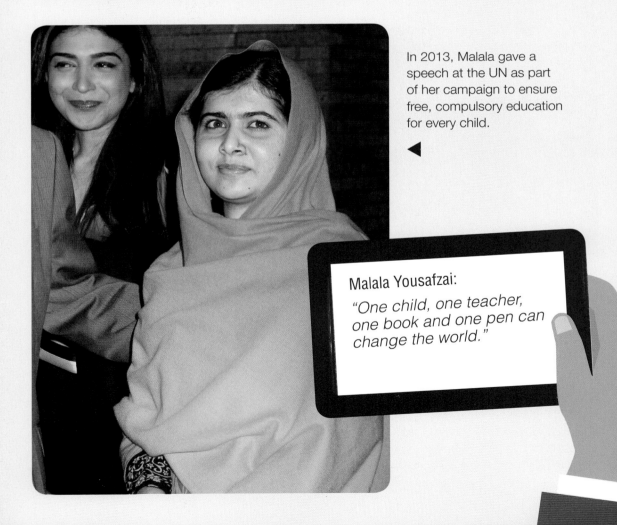

In 2013, Malala gave a speech at the UN as part of her campaign to ensure free, compulsory education for every child.

◀

Malala Yousafzai:

"One child, one teacher, one book and one pen can change the world."

Malala had a meeting with then-President Obama
in 2013 to thank him for the work of the U.S. in supporting
education in Pakistan.   ▼

Death Threats

Malala and her father, Ziauddin Yousafzai, were passionate about the
right for education. Malala's father ran a school and spoke out against
the Taliban. He was told by the Taliban that he had to close his school.
They both received death threats but continued to speak out about
the right for education, especially for girls. In 2012, Malala was shot in
the head by Taliban gunmen. British doctors in Pakistan were brought
in to help save Malala's life. Fiona Reynolds is an intensive care
specialist who had been asked to help. Fiona was scared about her
safety in this region of Pakistan. But she said, "Malala had been shot
because she wanted an education, and I was in Pakistan because
I'm a woman with an education, so I couldn't say no."

Malala survived and has continued to speak out about the right
to education.

Chapter 4

WHAT'S BEYOND THE HEADLINES ABOUT WOMEN'S RIGHTS?

Throughout history, women have had fewer rights, just because they were women. Women are less likely to be able to follow their free will. They are more likely to be controlled by parents or husbands. Women are less likely to have decision-making powers within a society and are more likely to live in poverty. Girls are less likely to receive an education. Without access to education, women don't have the same opportunities to earn money. Without education, they may not know how best to look after themselves and their families, putting lives at risk. Around the world, there are more women farmers than men but women rarely own the land they work on. This means that the profits from their work go to someone else.

American women fighting for the right to vote, 1915

THINK ABOUT IT

Women don't have the same equality in politics. In 2015, there were only 19 female heads of state or government. Yet research has found that when women hold political positions more laws that protect the environment are introduced. What do you think? Should women have more opportunities to hold political positions? What might be preventing women from holding these positions?

Unequal Treatment

Rights for women are improving, but women are still not treated equally. For example, women in Saudi Arabia are unable to travel or marry without the permission of a male guardian. This is usually her father or husband but it could be her son. In 2015, laws were changed in Saudi Arabia so divorced women and widows can now manage their family affairs without male approval.

Women are not allowed to drive in Saudi Arabia. Only men are allowed to have driving licences. ▶

New Zealand	1893
Australia	1902
Finland	1906
Norway	1913
Former Soviet Union (now Russia)	1917
Canada, Germany, Austria, Poland	1918
The United States, Hungary	1920
Great Britain	1918 and 1928
Myanmar	1922
Ecuador	1929
South Africa	1930
Brazil, Uruguay, Thailand	1932
Turkey, Cuba	1934
The Philippines	1937
France, Italy, Romania, China	1945
India	1949
Pakistan	1956
Syria	1973

This table shows where and when women won the right to vote.

◀

GOOD NEWS

In Botswana in 2012, a judge overturned a law which prevented women from inheriting property, saying that it's "an unacceptable system of male domination."

Violence Against Women and Girls

Violence against women is an important issue in both rich and poor countries. A UN study has found that one-third of women around the world have experienced some form of physical or sexual violence in their lifetime. More than 60 percent of these women didn't seek help. Much of this violence towards women happens at home but it also happens in public spaces. If women don't feel safe, they are less likely to access learning opportunities or leisure activities.

Female Genital Mutilation

Female genital mutilation (FGM), or "cutting," is when a girl or woman has all or part of her external genital organs removed for non-medical reasons. FGM is a sign of gender inequality. The UN is campaigning to put an end to this practice, which can cause health problems and even death. Surgical procedures can help reverse FGM but it may be difficult for women to seek such treatment. The UN estimates that at least 200 million women and girls have undergone FGM. The majority of these girls had it done to them before they were 5 years old. The UN are concerned that this practice still happens in 30 countries.

Special knives, pieces of glass, or razor blades may be used to perform FGM. Anaesthetics and antiseptics are not usually used.

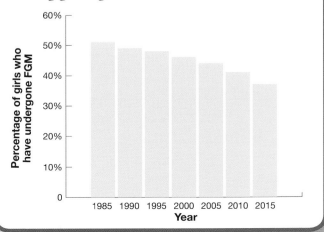

GOOD NEWS

This table shows the reduction in FGM among girls aged 15 to 19.

Child Marriages

In some cultures, it is the custom for girls to be married before they are 18 years old. This often occurs because the bride's family is poor and it means one less person to look after. There are more than 700 million women who were married as children. Of these women, 250 million were married before they were 15 years old. Getting married while still a child means that girls are less likely to continue with their education. They are also more likely to experience violence at home. Young teenage girls are more likely to have complications with pregnancy and childbirth too.

Bangladesh has the highest rate of marriage of girls under 15 years old.

Forced Marriages

A forced marriage is one where one or both people have not freely agreed to getting married. People may be physically threatened or abused or emotionally blackmailed to make them take part. Forced marriages are more common in South Asia. Sometimes young people are told that they are going to visit family. When they get there, it is actually to take part in their own marriage. Their family may have taken away their passports and so they are trapped and cannot get home.

Dowries

Historically, in many cultures it is traditional for a bride's family to give the groom's family a dowry. This is a payment for the cost of looking after the bride. A dowry could be a gift, money, goods, or property. However, sometimes the groom's family demands more and may use violence, or the threat of it, to try to get more. Dowry-related violence is most common in India, Pakistan, Sri Lanka, and Bangladesh. Violence against women includes physical beatings, rape, and starvation. Sometimes members of the groom's family may try to kill the wife. They may make it look like a suicide or an accident with a stove.

Viewpoint:

Amena, 17, thought she and her dad were going to visit her sick grandfather in Afghanistan. But when she got there, her dad told her that she was to marry her first cousin. She had never met this man, who was 10 years older than her. She felt sick and told her dad she didn't want to marry her cousin. She wanted to go home and back to school. Her dad said that it had all been arranged years ago and she had no choice. She was able to call her teacher who contacted the police and got her back home to her mother.

GOOD NEWS

In 2007, the United Kingdom added laws to protect people from forced marriages and to help those already in one.

If dowry demands are not met, some women have acid thrown at them. This Bangladeshi woman survived such an attack. ▼

Women in Rural Tanzania

In many cultures, it is traditional for women to be responsible for unpaid care work. This often means they are unable to access education or paid work. Without paid work, women are unable to improve their levels of poverty. They are reliant on family support. To break this cycle of poverty, women need opportunities to receive fairly paid work.

These women are working at a solar workshop in Tilonia, India. They are learning how to make solar lanterns. ▼

A division of the UN called UN Women is trying to break this cycle of poverty by providing training for women. If women can learn new skills that help them to earn money, then whole families can benefit. For example, the UN and India-based education organization Barefoot College arranged for a group of women from Tanzania to go to India for training. They spent six months learning how to install and maintain solar panels. They then returned home with the necessary knowledge and equipment to set up a solar electricity system for their villages.

Whole Community Benefit

The whole community can benefit from the knowledge these female engineers have brought back. Before their training, the women's small villages had no electricity. At night it would be dark or people had to use expensive (and dangerous) kerosene lights. Now they have a renewable and sustainable source of power. Children can do their homework under the solar lights. Women feel safer because most people now have lights outside their homes that act like streetlights.

The Way the Scheme Works

Villagers who want to take part in the scheme pay for the cost of the equipment and its maintenance over five years. Out of these funds, the engineers are paid a monthly wage for their work. The scheme has not only brought power to a community but has increased women's independence.

Chapter 5

WHAT'S BEYOND THE HEADLINES ABOUT EQUAL RIGHTS?

Human rights include the right not to be discriminated against because of race, religion, gender, or disability. One of the driving forces behind the introduction of the Universal Declaration of Human Rights (UDHR) was the events of World War II. People were persecuted because of their religion, race, sexuality, and disability.

Education plays an important part in religious tolerance.

Religious Persecution

Throughout history, religious persecution has taken place and, sadly, this kind of persecution continues around the world. For example, Rohingya Muslims have been persecuted for years in the mainly Buddhist country of Myanmar.

THINK ABOUT IT

Four days after the 9/11 attacks in 2001, Balbir Singh Sodhi was shot as he planted flowers in front of his store. He had nothing to do with the 9/11 attacks but was killed because he wore a turban. Why is it important that people should be able to follow their faith without persecution?

As well as persecution, people of different faiths may find that they are discriminated against in everyday life. They may be treated differently at school or not given a job because of what they believe in. Terror attacks by Islamic extremists have increased tensions between Muslims and other religions. Muslims are experiencing discrimination even though they do not hold the same extreme beliefs as these terrorists.

Trying to Make a Change

There are also positive examples of people trying to show they are happy to live side by side. In 2016, people in a village in Pakistan tried to bring people together and bring peace to their community. Seven years ago, religious mobs in the area attacked four churches and the houses of Christians, killing 10 people. Now the mainly Muslim community is showing solidarity by donating money and labor to help rebuild their Christian community's chapel.

In July 2016, people took to London's streets in campaigning for zero tolerance of racism and hate crime. ▼

Racial Equality

People have been discriminated against throughout history because of their race or ethnicity. The **civil rights** movement in the U.S. in the 1950s and 1960s provides a good example of this. In 1865, slavery was abolished in the U.S. African Americans were then supposed to have equal rights under the law but racial discrimination remained strong. Laws making it difficult for African Americans remained in place. Racial **segregation** was part of everyday life. The ongoing discrimination led to the civil rights movement. By the 1960s, protest marches and demonstrations were held around the country. Then, in 1963, police used high-pressure water hoses and dogs against students who were peacefully demonstrating. This shocking sight really got the country's attention. U.S. President John F. Kennedy said:

"We preach freedom around the world, and we mean it, and we cherish our freedom here at home, but are we to say to the world, and much more importantly, to each other that this is the land of the free except for the Negroes; that we have no second-class citizens except Negroes; that we have no class or caste system, no ghettoes, no master race except with respect to Negroes?"

The poor treatment of peaceful protestors by police in the 1960s encouraged more protestors to join the fight for racial equality.

India's Caste System

Traditional societies in India believe that people are born into different groups called castes. Some castes are considered better than others. Which caste a person belongs to depends on where they were born and what their parents do. People in the lower castes would be discriminated against.

GOOD NEWS

In 1920, Kocheril Raman Narayanan was born into India's lowest caste, called the "untouchables" or Dalits. His family was very poor and it was unthinkable that he would grow up to become India's president. Yet in 1997, he did just that.

Kocheril Raman Narayanan was India's tenth president. He held office from 1997 to 2002.

Disability Rights

There are many ways a person could have a disability. For example, they could have a physical or mental condition that means their movement is limited. Or they may have a visual or hearing **impairment**. There are one billion people in the world with some form of disability. About 93 million of these people are children.

In some parts of the world, people see a disability as something to hide. Families hide away children with disabilities. This means there could be more people than we know about.

Poverty and Disability

Poverty and disability are closely linked. People with a disability should be treated equally but they are often discriminated against. They are more likely to have less education, poorer health outcomes, lower levels of employment, and higher poverty rates. People with disabilities are often the poorest members of the population. They are at higher risk of physical

abuse and often don't receive proper nutrition. They face daily difficulties such as lack of suitable transportation and inaccessible buildings.

Poverty can also bring on disability from poor nutrition, lack of clean water and basic sanitation, or poor healthcare. Once disabled, people are more likely to be denied basic resources and so slip deeper into poverty.

◄

In some cultures, people with a disability are not given equal opportunities for employment and may end up begging on streets.

GOOD NEWS

The Paralympics show that people with a disability can achieve incredible feats and inspire us all. British swimmer Ellie Simmonds won two gold medals in her first Paralympics when she was just 13 years old. South African swimmer Achmat Hassiem lost his leg in a shark attack. Not only has he competed in the Paralympics, he also devotes time to shark conservation.

▲ Ellie Simmonds

Trying to Change

The UN, worldwide governments, and charities are trying to improve the quality of life for people with disabilities. They are creating inclusive policies, enforcing and updating laws, and putting in place appropriate support services. They are working with communities around the world to try to remove the discrimination connected to disability.

Famous physicist Steven Hawking:

"Disability need not be an obstacle to success. I have had motor neurone disease for practically all my adult life. Yet it has not prevented me from having a prominent career in astrophysics and a happy family life."

Hanif

Children with disabilities can be regarded by some as inferior. Hanif's story shows that, with proper support, people with disabilities can be effective in society.

▲ Educating others about people with a disability is important to prevent discrimination.

DID YOU KNOW?

The World Health Organization estimates that one billion people around the world live with a disability. At least 1 in 10 of these people are children and 80 percent live in developing countries.

A Life-Changing Injury

Hanif lives in a small village in Bangladesh. He was just 4 years old when he got injured while he was playing. His leg became red and swollen and he was in pain. His parents took him to the nearest hospital but doctors couldn't save his leg and had to amputate it.

After Hanif lost his leg, the other children were very mean to him. They pushed him to the floor and called him names. Hanif's parents wanted him to start school but Hanif couldn't walk the short distance to get there. Instead, his father had to carry him there. His father started a small shop selling tea near the school. This meant he could be there to carry Hanif home at the end of the day. The children at school were no kinder than those around his home so he continued to be bullied. He felt like he was inferior to the other children.

Then one day Hanif got good news. A charity in Dhaka, the capital of Bangladesh, would give him an artificial leg. People were so surprised to see Hanif walking and neighbors came to visit just to see his leg.

With his leg, Hanif can join in with the other children. They no longer call him names or push him around. Hanif feels more independent and is doing better at school. He hopes to be a teacher when he grows up.

Estimated Rates of Primary School Completion in Children with Disabilities

Boys with disability
51%

Girls with disability
42%

Boys without disability
61%

Girls without disability
53%

Refugees

Refugees are people who have been forced to flee their homes. They may have fled because of the dangers of conflict, **persecution**, generalized violence, or human rights **violations**. At the end of 2015, the number of people forced from their homes had reached 65.3 million. That's the highest number ever recorded. This number is made up of refugees, **asylum** seekers, or **internally displaced** people. Migrant workers are sometimes grouped in with displaced people. But migrant workers are choosing to move because they want to find work, not because of conflict or natural disaster.

Top 10 Origins of People Applying for Asylum in the EU

Pakistan 45,000
Eritrea 40,000
Nigeria 35,000
Iran 28,000
Ukraine 23,000

Syria 360,000

Albania 60,000

Kosovo 70,000

Iraq 120,000

Afghanistan 158,000

Nizar, 5 years old:

"The bombers came and destroyed our house. They shot fire, and destroyed my toys. They didn't leave a single piece of them."

Where to Go?

A refugee has the same human rights as everyone else. They also have the right to be in a safe place. This is sometimes difficult to ensure. The number of people forced to flee can cause a crisis. Refugees may have fled very quickly, bringing only the things they could carry. They need food and housing and to be able to rebuild their lives. Organizations such as charities and the UN set up camps for displaced people. These camps offer aid to people but are only short-term solutions. The UN would prefer people to settle in communities where they can use their skills to make a living. However, neighboring countries may be flooded with people. Other countries are put under pressure to help by welcoming more refugees. Racial tension and conflict can increase under this pressure. Safeguarding the human rights of refugees is a big challenge for all those involved.

GOOD NEWS

The billionaire George Soros, who survived Nazi occupation during World War II, has given $500 million to charities who help migrants and refugees.

Many Syrians have become ▲ refugees in their attempt to escape the violence of the Syrian civil war.

Refugee Stories

When children become refugees, their education is severely affected, if not stopped altogether. The UN estimates that half of primary-school-age refugees are not in school. However, the UN are trying to get children back into education. For example, refugees from the Syrian civil war are being helped by 50 different agencies. These agencies are trying to help as many children as possible to continue with their education.

DID YOU KNOW?

One in every 113 people in the world is a refugee.

▲ The UN's refugee agency, UNHCR, uses a ferry to transport refugees from Ivory Coast.

Mahmoud's Story

Nine-year-old Mahmoud and his family had to flee Syria in 2012 because of the war. They spent two years in Egypt where he was unable to go to school. He was scared to leave his home because he was bullied and beaten for being Syrian. Mahmoud's parents made a very difficult decision. They sent him on his own on an illegal boat to Italy in the hope he would find a better life. It was a terrifying time for him. The boat was shot at and returned to Egypt. Eventually Mahmoud was reunited with his family.

The UN's agency for refugees helped Mahmoud's family to find a safe place to live. They were told that Sweden had agreed that they could live there. Mahmoud was delighted to be traveling to start a new life instead of to escape the old one. He was happy to attend school, and quickly learned enough Swedish to help him make friends.

DID YOU KNOW?

In 2015, there were 98,400 children who were not with parents or family and needed a safe place to live.

THINK ABOUT IT

Think about how desperate Mahmoud's parents must have been to want to send their young child alone to another country.

What Can You Do?

Human rights is a complex issue. There are international laws designed to protect everyone, regardless of their race, religion, language, gender, or disability. However, there are people around the world who don't respect these rights. Perhaps some people don't even know these rights exist. Education is vital in providing and protecting human rights. Everyone can play a part by finding out more about these issues and helping others to understand them too. The more people who know about human rights, the more people who can help protect human rights.

You could find out about a charity that supports human rights issues ▲ you are interested in. Perhaps you could think about setting up events to help raise funds and awareness for your chosen issue.

Learn from the Past

Learning about human rights issues in the past, such as the horrific consequences of allowing or ignoring discrimination against people because of their religion, can help us to understand why human rights are so important now. We can also learn about human potential and the good that comes from respecting each other.

Keep Up-to-date

Keeping up with current events can help people understand the problems of others. Try to find out both sides of the issue. For example, in 2016, European countries were closing their borders to refugees. They were afraid of the number of people and what it might do to their countries. Some people were worried that terrorists could be hidden within these numbers. On the other hand, refugees say they are just people looking for peace. As Mohamed Ahmed from Syria says, "We are not a danger, we are humans. We are coming from wars and we just want to start a new life."

World Refugee Day is celebrated on June 20 every year to raise awareness for the plight of refugees.

Human rights cover all areas of life and are a massive global challenge. Some issues, such as the treatment of women, are firmly established in cultures going back centuries. Organizations such as the UN are trying to transform the world by putting an end to poverty and hunger. They want people to be able to live with equal rights and in a healthy environment. By working hard to encourage and provide education, people can benefit from skills and knowledge. They can earn a living and raise themselves out of poverty. Education and tolerance of others can help prevent the spread of conflict and terror.

Attracting Attention

Attracting attention to important human rights issues can help make a difference. In 2010, the UN created a branch focused specifically on the empowerment of women. This showed the importance of gender equality, not only as a basic human right but also because empowering women can help economies to grow. The treatment of people with disabilities needs to remain a priority, as these quotes from children with disabilities show:

"We need to believe in ourselves and challenge negative opinions by showing how able we are."

"Disability is in the eyes of society. It is not in our eyes. If provided with opportunities, we can prove our worth."

GOOD NEWS

The Western Wall in Jerusalem is one of Judaism's most holy sites. For decades, women were not allowed to pray alongside men. But in January 2016, the Israeli government approved the creation of an official area for mixed gender prayer.

Protecting children from war and conflict has to remain a priority for the world. ▼

Working Together

By working together and keeping informed, people can try to prevent future conflicts happening. If there's peace in the world, people can put their efforts into improving lives.

TIMELINE

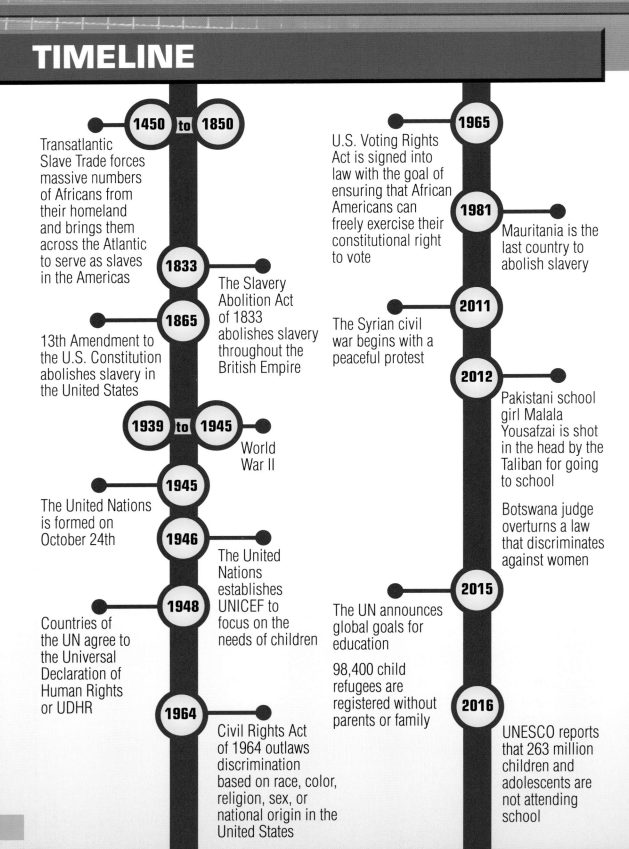

1450 to **1850**

Transatlantic Slave Trade forces massive numbers of Africans from their homeland and brings them across the Atlantic to serve as slaves in the Americas

1833

The Slavery Abolition Act of 1833 abolishes slavery throughout the British Empire

1865

13th Amendment to the U.S. Constitution abolishes slavery in the United States

1939 to **1945**

World War II

1945

The United Nations is formed on October 24th

1946

The United Nations establishes UNICEF to focus on the needs of children

1948

Countries of the UN agree to the Universal Declaration of Human Rights or UDHR

1964

Civil Rights Act of 1964 outlaws discrimination based on race, color, religion, sex, or national origin in the United States

1965

U.S. Voting Rights Act is signed into law with the goal of ensuring that African Americans can freely exercise their constitutional right to vote

1981

Mauritania is the last country to abolish slavery

2011

The Syrian civil war begins with a peaceful protest

2012

Pakistani school girl Malala Yousafzai is shot in the head by the Taliban for going to school

Botswana judge overturns a law that discriminates against women

2015

The UN announces global goals for education

98,400 child refugees are registered without parents or family

2016

UNESCO reports that 263 million children and adolescents are not attending school

GLOSSARY

asylum—protection given to refugees from another country, often for political reasons

civil rights—the rights that all people have to freedom and equal treatment under the law

concentration camp—a camp where people such as prisoners of war, political prisoners, or refugees are held under harsh conditions

extremist—a person whose views or actions are far beyond the norm

genocide—deliberate killing of a large group of people, especially with the intention to destroy a particular ethnic group

internally displaced—people who have been forced to flee their homes but who have stayed in their own country

persecution—cruel or unfair treatment, often because of race or religious beliefs

philosopher—a person who studies ideas, the way people think, and the search for knowledge

plantation—a large farm where crops such as cotton and sugarcane are grown. Before 1865, plantations in the U.S. were run by slave labor

segregation—practice of separating people of different races, income classes, or ethnic groups

United Nations (UN)—a group of countries that works together for peace and security

violation—an action that breaks a rule or a law

widow—a woman whose spouse has died and who has not remarried

World War II—a war in which the United States, France, Great Britain, the Soviet Union, and other countries defeated Germany, Italy, and Japan; World War II lasted from 1939 to 1945

National news websites and newspapers are a good way of keeping up-to-date with the latest information about topical issues.

Places to visit

Museums and memorials around the world help keep memories alive.

www.jewishmuseum.org.uk/Home
Jewish Museum, London

www.nationalholocaustcentre.net
The National Holocaust Centre and Museum, Nottinghamshire

Websites

Use Facthound to find Internet sites related to this book.

Here's all you do:
Visit *www.facthound.com*

Just type in 9781484641415 and go!

Books

Brown, Dinah. *Who Is Malala Yousafzai? Who Is...?*
New York: Grosset and Dunlap, 2015.

Freeburg, Jessica. *Fight for Survival: The Story of the Holocaust.*
Tangled History. North Mankato, Minn.: Capstone Press, 2017.

Senker, Cath. *Stephen Hawking.* Against the Odds.
Chicago: Heinemann Raintree, 2015.

Throp, Claire. *Malala Yousafzai.* Against the Odds.
Chicago: Heinemann Raintree, 2015.

INDEX